Retrievals

Retrievals

Collected Poems

by
Tim Wenzell

RESOURCE *Publications* • Eugene, Oregon

RETRIEVALS
Collected Poems

Copyright © 2020 Tim Wenzell. All rights reserved. Except for brief quotations in critical publications or reviews, no part of this book may be reproduced in any manner without prior written permission from the publisher. Write: Permissions, Wipf and Stock Publishers, 199 W. 8th Ave., Suite 3, Eugene, OR 97401.

Resource Publications
An Imprint of Wipf and Stock Publishers
199 W. 8th Ave., Suite 3
Eugene, OR 97401

www.wipfandstock.com

PAPERBACK ISBN: 978-1-7252-5544-9
HARDCOVER ISBN: 978-1-7252-5545-6
EBOOK ISBN: 978-1-7252-5546-3

Manufactured in the U.S.A.   JANUARY 7, 2020

For Louise, for my continuing journey with her

Contents

Acknowledgements | ix

What You've Let In | 1
Wrong Answers, a Catholic school sonnet | 2
Retrieval | 3
Times Tables | 5
Coat Room | 6
Sinistry | 7
May Procession Practice | 9
Shoes (Global Warming Version) | 12
Further Notes on the Spiders of New Guinea | 14
Here for the Food | 16
A Cat Dies | 18
Another Cat Dies (same way) | 20
Campfire Reading | 21
Pinball at Garby's | 22
Overlook | 24
Inhale | 25
Ellen | 26
Asbury Park, December | 27
Mike falling, late Sixties | 28
Cedar Chest | 30
Day Coming | 32

Elvis | 34

Discoverers | 35

Light Crack Beneath Doorway, 3 a.m. | 36

Anthony | 37

Child of Divorce at a Wedding | 41

The Reason for Ceilings | 43

Mrs. Albertson at 59 | 44

Midnight, 662 Ashmont, 413 Elder, 12 Barley, 1555 Sinkler, and on | 45

Selkirk's Bus Yard, 3 a.m. | 46

Argument on a Clam | 48

Basement, 442 Claire | 49

Corona-Lookers Anonymous | 50

Sulphur City | 51

Forgotten Spot | 52

Pink | 53

Big Disappointment | 55

Stopping Off | 57

Poverty, Inc. | 59

Recycle Day | 61

The History of Lost Game Shows | 63

The Tavern Keeper at the Edge of the World | 67

Wanted: One-Inch Baby Jesus | 69

Signal School | 70

Acknowledgements

"Campfire Reading" previously published in *The Comstock Review*. Spring 1998. Vol. 12 No. 1: 87. Print.

"Coat Room" previously published in *Poetry Super Highway*. September 2015. Web. http://poetrysuperhighway.com/psh/2015/09/september-21-27-2015-john-tustin-and-tim-wenzell/

"Discoverers" previously published in *Black Bear Review*. #36, spring-summer 2003: 22. Print.

"Ellen" previously published in *Adelaide Literary Magazine*, Year III, Number 18, November 2018. Print and Web.

"Further Notes on the Spiders of New Guinea" previously published in *Adelaide Literary Magazine*, Year III, Number 18, November 2018. Print and Web.

"Here for the Food" previously published in *Adelaide Literary Magazine*, Year III, Number 18, November 2018. Print and Web.

"Asbury Park, December" previously published in *Haikuniverse*. http://www.haikuniverse.com/haiku-by-tim-wenzell/. July 8, 2018. Web.

"Inhale" previously published in *Squidink*. #3 2003: 7. Print.

"Light Crack Beneath Doorway, 3 a.m." previously published in *Black Bear Review*. #36, spring-summer 2003: 22. Print.

"May Procession Practice" previously published in *Cleaver Magazine*. Issue 13. March 2016. http://www.cleavermagazine.com/may-procession-practice-by-timothy-wenzell/. Web.

"Mike Falling, Late Sixties" previously published in *Curbside Review*. Volume 1, Issue 9. September 2000: 4. Print.

"Nine" previously published in *Black Bear Review*, Spring/Summer 2003: 22. Print.

"Nine Times Tables" previously published in *Falling Star Magazine*. 2016. Print.

"Overlook" previously published in *Squidink*. #3 2003: 6. Print.

"Pinball at Garby's" previously published in *Rearview Quarterly*. Summer 2003. Volume 2, issue 2: 21-22. Print.

"Shoes (Global Warming Version)" previously published in *Adelaide Literary Magazine*, Year III, Number 18, November 2018. Print and Web.

"A Cat Dies" previously published in *Adelaide Literary Magazine*, Year III, Number 18, November 2018. Print and Web.

"Times Tables" previously published in *Poetry Super Highway*. September 2015. Web.

http://poetrysuperhighway.com/psh/2015/09/september-21-27-2015-john-tustin-and-tim-wenzell/

"What You've Let In" previously published in *Stirring: A Literary Collection*. August 2000. Web. http://www.sundress.net/stirring/archives/v2/e9/wenzellt.htm.

"Wrong Answers" previously published in *Poetry Super Highway*. September 2015. Web. http://poetrysuperhighway.com/psh/2015/09/september-21-27-2015-john-tustin-and-tim-wenzell/

What You've Let In

The flight of the wasp
circling in wide arcs
across the length of the sagging ceiling
startles you from your straw chair and
gets you to thinking:

"I should not open the porch door
merely to gaze across the dying hedges
at the fresh coat of dew
settled
upon the tin roofs."

Wrong Answers, a Catholic school sonnet

I wasn't certain of square roots and things
Sister Joseph threatened we'd better know
for the oral exam she said would show
our little ears who were those studying
our decimals and fraction lines: dividing
large into small, endless digits below
zero. I tried hiding in that back row
from her stare, waiting for that bell to ring.

Sister Joseph eyed my crouch right away,
hiding with my long, jumbled numbers in
my head. She rained tough problems down on me,
full of evil intention. "Don't dare say
a thing," I told me, "hold your silence. Sin
walks down the aisle, with zero mercy."

Retrieval

They steal your pencil cases
was the first thing I told my mother
on the first afternoon
I came home
from first grade.

well you can't let that happen
was what my father told me
as he clipped my tie on
my second morning
after my toast.

On the second day
in the second aisle
I saw my pencil case
sitting on a desk
of a tall boy called James.
I reached from my aisle
for my pencil case
but he held tight so
I pulled and pulled until
the tall boy and his desk

came crashing down in a sea
of papers and pencils
and catechisms.

"why are you hanging ten feet in the air
from a coat hook?"
my father asked me
after my second day
and during my first detention.
I told him
Sister simply hung me here
for trying to get back
what was mine.

Times Tables

Being W
they put me
in the ninth row
second to last
in front of Maria Zimmerman.

A is easy, ones and two times twos
but nine times sevens and nine times nines
come down the aisle of V's and W's and Y's

Wait this isn't fair to think so much more
sixty-two no sixty-four or wait is it sixty-five
with rows of eyes turned backward
to you as you finally answer dead wrong
and Sister sends you to the coat room
to collect your proper thoughts.

Coat Room

Through the partition window
the light showed me
several blackbirds
putting themselves
upon the iron railing going down,
one of them looking beady-eyed up
through the partition,
eyeballing me trapped
in the coat room.

It smelled like suffocating camphor
and the bulb flickered cold
when Sister shut off the light,
leaving only the dark strangulation and
the little pencil of sunlight
peering through the partition window
onto Miriam Mackey's red tweed.

"Sister get me out of here
I'm ready to learn some Math again"
I whispered through the wall
as the boys in the last row
recited their nine-times tables.

Sinistry

You are writing with the hand of the devil
Sister Dominicus
Margaret
Mary
Francis
Josephite
Corpus Christi
whispered
into that ear of mine
she had pinched
with her heavy holy Godfingers
knashing her teeth while
hanging and twisting her cross
in the air above my desk.

I wanted to crawl
into my empty wooden inkwell as
the right-handers looked back
with their dead left arms
eyeballing
Sister Dominicus
Margaret

Mary
Josephite
Corpus Christi
putting a pen
into my God-hand telling me
"Now all good Catholics stay between the lines."

May Procession Practice

Little I stand by William
at the crest of the asphalt hill
looking into the incinerator,
watching the chocolate milk cartons burn while
shaking away my need to piss.

Mother Phoebe has just told the tall boys
at the bottom of the asphalt hill
how to turn like soldiers and
she looks across the ballyard
to the white church
with open doors leading
all the way to Jesus
hanging with His thorny crown over

candles dripping wax hot wax
running down the sides as
my piss leaks
down my trousers like
wax hot wax.

A yellow stream
slithers snakelike

with its foamy head,
gathering momentum downhill
to Sanctuary
between Mother's feet and
breaking her stare from
those sacred flames.

Chocolate milk cartons burn and burn,
incinerating into black feathers rising
out through the carbon chimney,
out of the inferno.

Mother Phoebe walks
up the yellow river to its source:
Hell comes quickly now
so God puts a Whisper into my ear:
"brush the puddle to William's leg
and say 'he pissed sister
he pissed sister.'"

But God in all His Glory
can't hide the wet stain
moonsize on my crotch
staring back at the big blue habit hovering,
a monolith with a silver cross
over me and my piss
and my hands done up in prayer.

Now the voice of God has gone away,
now the cartons have burned to ash,
now I'm just waiting
for the Iron Hand of Mother
(getting ready to come down).

Shoes (Global Warming Version)

A true woman evacuates with her shoes
and makes certain that all of them,
wrapped in garbage bags,
fill the trunk so that
he will take the back seat with his things
(whatever those might be).

The Artimus river
broke two dams and the St. Sebastian walls
with their ivy, their moss, and their history,
and dropped them to the sludgy bottom.
The mud rose in clumps and fell along the banks
like vanished turtles,
dotting the shorelines when the rain let up
and producing some kind of landscape:
torn chunks of houses, diminished chimneys,
and brown wet sofas
falling back into earth.

They will never build here again
and in a thousand years, or maybe five hundred,
(or maybe tomorrow)

when the oceans converge into a thick salt sludge
filling like a hardening glue
into the spaces that are left
a true woman will open her trunk
and pick out just the right shoes
for the occasion.

Further Notes on the Spiders of New Guinea

Do invertebrates dream?
For example,
does the Brain coral dream
it is a human brain
inside a skull, looking out
through land-rooted eyes at
a world beyond
the bottom of its sea?

What about the Bay Ghost shrimp
dreaming of being real?
or the Aggregating anemone
wishing in sleep to finally be calm?

What about the Cave cricket
chirping in its sleep for daylight?
or the Missouri millipede
walking upright in a dream
on just two legs?

Does a House spider drift off
after the lights have been turned down?

Where to? The deep forest where lights
never click on, where webs are
never swept away by brooms?

In the deep sleep of an earth
alive with everything,
I would like to think that house spiders
can weave webs that rise
into the upper canopies of rain forests,
fabulous filaments so graceful and long
that they disappear into Whitmanesque infinity:
no tears, no slamming of doors, no shouting,
no brooms, no lights to go down.

Instead, it is a party of the living,
day and night, with the company of other dreamers:
The ant colonies marching in, the beetles crawling home,
the crescendo of the crickets, loud and long,
and the dark, iridescent and beautiful spiders,
massed together with webs open and
lying in wait for everything to awaken.

Here for the Food

My father left his family
in the middle of a cold night in 1933.
He said he was going out for coal.
That was two years ago
and on the day I turned twelve:

Now I am the man of the house and we must eat,
so I am here for the food.
I understand your mother died, and I feel for that.
She must have been a wonderful woman, raising such mourners.
I see her there up at the altar in her fancy box
so I will file in line and cry for her with you.

But I really need your reception
more than anything.
You will have a spread, after all.
I brought my pants with the large pockets
to fill with finger foods
while I fill your world with lies
about how I knew her:
Yes, I will say between bites, she was like a mother to me.
And if you knew the truth instead of the lie I have provided,
you would understand why I am taking your little ham sandwiches.

I saw my father yesterday.
Gaunt and out of a car,
he walked across the baseball field
and handed me a dollar bill
while I stood on second base.

But I did not know that I had seen him
until I went home and described
the shadow-stranger to my mother.
She handled the dollar in her hands,
unsure of where to pass it.
(But I am a man and I can rise above
her trembling and her stare into space,
and I will use that dollar if she doesn't).

I check the obits,
and another rich one has died,
this time an old man down on Devoe.
So here I will be again in my little blue suit
and working up a good cry,
rehearsing the right lines
in the back pew
about their beautiful grandfather,
their father, their friend and
"a great man who helped me
find my way."

A Cat Dies

I am crying:
Speckles has been hit by a truck,
thrown into underbrush by rolling tires,
and I am standing in the roadside dust
watching the truck disappear into a wall of thick air.
And where are my mother and father?

I am six and angry. They have just told me
that I can't watch the Flintstones
because I will stay awake and stare at my ceiling
and have bad dreams about a barefooted Fred
locked outside by the cat all night.

I am seven now, not six,
no longer worried about Fred knocking
for Wilma, not after the non-cartoon cat I hold in my hands
looks into space and knows
that someone seven and crying, or six and angry,
won't be able to save it.
And where are my mother and father?

This is the windiest day I remember:
The dirt arrives in little tornadoes at my feet and

a cold invisible wall pushes against me
and my suddenly still Speckles
locked inside my arms
on the side of the road.

The light disappears.
Fred won't wait out there forever—
Wilma will open the prehistoric door,
stop his shouting, allow him to finally lay down
on his stone bed and sleep, and in the morning
I can bury Speckles on the opposite side of the pool.
But where are my mother and father
with the shovel?

Another Cat Dies (same way)

Witnessing the death of a cat
at the age of nine, a cat
caught in the wheels of a car
and carried by the centrifugal force
into some lady's bushes in a blurry ball of
cat fur, and me, me
carried by the centrifugal force
of my spinning heartbeats that carry
my hands around a cat dying, dying, then
dead, dead in my arms that makes me
go from nine to one hundred
and nine because the world
is suddenly a jolt from a power line
and the world of nine no longer
fits a pattern where cats live
when they get run over
just like that,
a pattern where they live
in your arms, they live
and they
just
don't
die there.

Campfire Reading

I listen to my brother tell his story
on the boulder across the fire.
I listen as his voice flickers in
and out of the black swamp ink
into a sea of sobbing frogs and
their aquatic catechisms.
I listen as his voice vibrates the ground
varnished by the long streaks
of dewed grass,
hair of the earth
warning us of morning.

I listen to his words—
knife-edge scrapes in the soundful barrier
falling, rising, falling,
rising into the faint gray ash sailing up and out
sailing to the stars, so many stars
so many sobbing frogs, so many catechisms.

Pinball at Garby's

I am a ten-year old trapped in a bar
with fifty cents and a wooden cross on a string
that Garby gave me to hold
until he finished his last game of pool.

They gave me enough soda and straws
and the coins in my hands are warm with metal sweat,
so I dismount the stool like a fireman
taking two babies and a cross to safety:

I want to put the quarters into the machine, but
I won't be able to get past the man draped in too many
beers
and one last shot there by the knobs,
he trying to balance himself and remember the door.

He is something like my father later in the night,
he is something like me later in the years,
he is something like everyone around me
as he holds the dust of Garby's between his beers,
the smell of its memories from the rest room walls,
the corner of a cocktail napkin on his left heel.

And me? I am bored and looking at the clock,
little hand moving toward two and little me
waiting for my father, bankrupt of certainty,
to finish talking and drinking his fatherhood away—
or for the man by the machine, feeling wind from the open door,
to fish his car keys from some pocket
and make for the dead highway.

I will clutch the wooden cross tight and pray to it,
pray for the moment the bar floor clears and
for an unfettered walk fifty cents
away,
a world behind heavy glass and arrived at
by perfect silver balls
setting off buzzing bells, glistening galaxies,
rows and rows of perfect lights that all
erupt in harmony and reward me with
two hundred fifty thousand points.

Overlook

I wish I had a chair
in the trunk of my car
so that when I saw
something
off to the side of the road
I could just pull out the chair
from the trunk of my car and
unfold it and sit down and
just watch
Something.

Inhale

The mentally battered man,
late in his forty-third summer,
runs along dead drunk
behind the bug spray truck
in an attempt to capture
ten years old in Lilac Lane when he, with
Jo-Jo and Davey and Carl and Reen and Bethy and Bobby,
Josey and Smitty and Shiloh
ran behind
the bug-spray truck in an attempt to take in
the fog that was killing the mosquitoes
swarming all about, the mosquitoes
swarming all about.

Ellen

She ran into herself
like a parakeet into a hall mirror
and couldn't fly for a while,
she of the missing make-up,
absent of pointed shoes mounted on racks
hanging from her closet door—
no fabrics hanging on wooden poles in veils of plastic,

confronted instead with a tape of her own voice
screaming at some hour, screaming
that seeped through walls
and under doors, woke neighbors,
deluding her finally from beauty.

Asbury Park, December

Winter seagulls wait
for the people of summer
and their bags of food.

Mike falling, late Sixties

The room beneath the broken drop ceiling
after Mike fell through
the fiberglass field
he thought he could walk on
was a room belonging to a house
in some other world

mom had just bought herself
a loud flowery bedspread
and lava lamp and
I'd never looked down on a room
from a broken drop ceiling
with Mike falling through
before

falling
like a stone
into a bed of cartoon flowers
wrapping their vines and their wisteria
and their dyed morning glories
around him as he twisted

to red lava
rising out of the nightstand:
Mike didn't know whether to look back up
from where he came
or to where he had arrived.

> *(I must have thought he arrived*
> *at a room*
> *on some distant planet*
> *below the universe of the attic)*

Cedar Chest

I

I sat legs up
on the wing-backed chair
beneath the peeling bannister
of grandmother's rowhome
the morning after
they lowered her
into the muddy earth
drinking the lemonade
she'd left in a pitcher
that tasted like yesterday.

My father brought the
Victorian mirror
with the ornate frame
down off the flowered wallpaper
that would be painted over
in a sterile white
by my father's roller;
he brought the mirror
down to the floor

and there it reflected
a flash of dead earth
on my heels

II

They gave me her cedar chest
to put at the bottom
of my bed,
the chest my father thought he had emptied
except I found the photograph
in a side pocket:
the picture that showed
my mother in the sand
with her pigtails tight
in a checkered sundress and
years removed from my conception.
She was holding out a hand
to my lipsticked grandmother
under a sepia sky.

Day Coming

Signaling the day to come
in the showered fusion
of blue starry wisps
the pounding currents
draw the shadow-sphere
into its waning gibbous
lowering itself
into the darkened room with you
and the buzz of dragonfly nests
on the pond shore.

Where does night trickle out?
the silence swims its course
on black sheets of spiny air
out of some enclosed vortex
of webbed violet whispering
"death is noise... life is silence"
in some secret tongue masked on the edge
of a distant echo
from that place between
sleep and awake.

You only half-listen
as day seeps through
and the robes beckon you
from the silver hook.

Elvis

The same night my hamster Elvis
died among the cedar chips
was the same night
the Shemanski brothers
took their LeSabre
over the bluff
and cracked through the ice
and sunk into Sally lake
with only a floating six-pack
to mark their spot.

> *Did you know that for every hamster that dies*
> *two humans die?*

Discoverers

You in the process of trying to
get lost, me
in the process of trying to
be found, you

Light Crack Beneath Doorway, 3 a.m.

The room where daddy makes monsters
sits just past the bathroom and the last light
in the hallway and filled
with sounds unearthly, sounds made from foil and speakers
and mud and spoons and
boxes of dead leaves and heavy wooden shoes and breathing,
heavy breathing that makes you think
and stay up
and think
that Unreal and Real
are only separated by
two letters.

Anthony

While hunting for snakes,
Anthony told me
about a hairy spider he saw
along the Neshaminy creek.
"A foot long and a foot wide,
coconut body."

"Ran into the web almost,
a web the size of bedsheets
stretched on clotheslines.
Spider spun it
just off the creek."

Anthony lost his life
in the back of a Voyager
that same November
while belted into the seat
facing the other way
out along the Beltway,
sitting no doubt
with a wide final gaze
as he watched the headlights

coming, coming,
hearing the mixed shouts
from the front seats
and then the thud of eternity.

Anthony weathered the thunderstorm
in the cabin tent
folded beside him
in the Voyager,
a tent still smelling
of field grass and campfire smoke,
still missing a support pole
and stakes.

I read on an inside page
of my father's Evening Bulletin
that Anthony lost his life
next to that folded cabin tent.
(And I saw the photo crinkled
at the bottom of the page,
black- and- white twisted Voyager,
darkness of night,
pebbles of glass in shiny puddles).

If Anthony had kept running
on that path
he would have hit
that bedsheet spider web
full-force on his face—

the needle legs would have
scrambled across Anthony
and the spider would have
dug into his forehead
with black angry fangs—

right to the Emergency room
they would have rushed him
in the Voyager,
Anthony and his father
tearing up the beltway,
driving Anthony
and his spider bite
to Cooper Medical,
right to the doctors
and their gauze.

"He's going to have a welt
the size of a golf ball,"
doctor would have whispered
behind the blue curtain
to Anthony's father.
"We'll keep him overnight
to make sure of things."

Anthony would have been sent to a bed
on the twenty-second floor
and he would have changed the world
by sleeping in that bed

that night:
he wouldn't have camped in a storm,
he wouldn't have been backwards
next to the cabin tent
on that November day.

Anthony! You should have kept running
down that path
to the waiting spider!
You would be alive!
(I could call you up and tell you
about the snake
that I just saw.
I could tell you about
the way it moved
like a black ripple
across the clearing).

Child of Divorce at a Wedding

A four-year old boy in a white shirt and red clip-on tie
stands in the men's room along the urinal wall
waiting for dad to finish throwing up in the first stall:

He is listening to the sound of seven shots and ten beers
and chicken capon coming up
out of suddenly strange dad,
but he is watching the men along the wall
piss into vertical toilets,
and the boy tries to straighten
his little red tie.

After the dance floor clears,
the music packed away in leather boxes
and the coats on hooks all but gone,
his grandfather will call into the stall,
carry his father away from the last peeing man,
drive the both of them home in his big car—

And the little boy will sleep over
his grandparents' house
in the room with the dusty crib

and the flickering night light,
and wait for Sunday drop-off
at his mother's high-rise.

The Reason for Ceilings

You'd better go inside now,
this you don't want to see or know about,
because then you'll have to feel all empty and small,
and humbled by those billion stars carved into galaxies,
infinite sentences begging for periods—
except if you want to call each star a period
and the sky one long and uneventful essay.

But even then, a star is too far away a place
to throw even a thought (even yours, even mine).

I know I will have trouble with this,
and I won't be able to sleep,
considering how insignificant I am,
and I will try to hide the image of stars
by burying my head into pillows
and wishing away such eternities.

I will have trouble with this
and so will you,
so you'd better go inside now.

Mrs. Albertson at 59

She fell asleep with a cigarette
between her ring fingers
snoring airplane decibels, so
sons and daughters knew
when to rise from beds
to come put out rug or mattress fires
or just to slip the cold butt
from between the rings
and drop it good night
into the ash tray.

Midnight, 662 Ashmont, 413 Elder, 12 Barley, 1555 Sinkler, and on

Old cats meow
at locked doors
because they don't
want to die in houses.
There is the decomposition of earth just past the
porch lights which call them,
and they in turn call for their masters to gather
keys to unlock and open
so that they may have the little time left
to lay down on immediate earth.

But their masters are deep in their houses
tending artificial fires
or basting game hens under fluorescent lights
or tuned to some channel and transfixed
by panthers ready to spring
or watching something furry and newborn
making its way
through the dead leaves.

Selkirk's Bus Yard, 3 a.m.

There is an acre of empty school buses
where the homeless children sleep,
there among the burned-out holes
of cylinders and pipes and
the magic-marker phone numbers
of long-dead girls
scrawled on the metal bars
of pea-green seats.

There behind the mud blankets of windshields,
they try to keep from falling
from their beds
to the floors of places
where once there were no such things
as sleep
or silence or
bookless children—
they are lying with no thoughts at all
of fractions in chalk.

The fog that rolls
across the chain linked fence

and into the bus yard
might be the heavy hand
of memory,
drifting and depositing
something
of what was.

Or it might be only fog
that hovers, that settles
as Safety finally
into each of their dreams
like a benediction.

Argument on a Clam

"It's psychological."
"It's slimy."

Basement, 442 Claire

The Stolzers had a lot of toys
I used to ask to stay,
I hung out with the Stolzer boys
just so I could play

with trucks and games and monster toys
the toys they said would stay
they'd stay there with the Stolzer boys
because they savored play.

The Stolzers have a lot of toys,
my memory will stay,
my memory of the Stolzer boys
and their eternal play.

Corona-Lookers Anonymous

Corona-Lookers Anonymous gather like door mice
in their unlit room beneath the steeple
huddled in a plastic-chaired circle
cursing their invisible sun,
cursing their common blindness.

Sulphur City

Gathered in small bunches and pressed body to body
the match-stick people look upright and out
through their glass column of a thousand reflections
Fearing the gas radiator
bleeding on the floor.

Forgotten Spot

The swelling river came up and finally washed his treasure
from the earth, baseball cards from the early sixties
and poems in pencil of mallards and things

Too far away he was to see the unearthed rusted box;
he could only hear the muffled rainfall on the hospital windows
as they fucked with his monitor.

Pink

The ultrasound technician thought she saw a penis
But it was only a developing thumb
glowing on the screen
and she gave a thumbs up,
seemingly at a boy.

They named him early, named him Seth;
the room was of cobalt blue,
with his father's footballs
and a framed letter from the president of Churchill Motors
on what it was like to become a man.

And the posters on the walls for Seth to absorb
from his burgeoning beginnings?
The surfers off waterfalls, the celebrated championship,
the mushroom cloud in the desert
they said killed John Wayne.

Then the birth canal producing a girl:
the world recoils, now what?
What of the blue, of the touchdowns,
of the play at the plate? What of the mushroom cloud
and what of the rising as a man in the world?

Now, dear, we must put away the surfboard
and tiptoe carefully over the top of the falls.
Avoid the desert air at all costs
and be safe in the knowledge
that pink cans of paint, posters of gardens,
and a framed letter from Sally's Finishing School
are on their way.

Big Disappointment

When Sethena saw them building the chimney,
she yelled it wasn't wide enough for Santa,
so it should come down.

They wiped their troughs and snickered down
while below the roof Sethena screamed
and sobbed into her new house.

They tried to console her fracturing world
but the fireplace told them it was just too small.

"The only thing we can do now that will solve this thing
is to have them widen the chimney."

So they brought in more mortar and made it wide enough
for a fat man on a cold night to ostensibly go down.

That first year all of the presents, even the assembled bicycle
under the decorated tree, made plain and perfect sense.

Then the cry from the back row in math class the following fall:
There is no Santa, there is no Santa, there is no Santa . . .

Then the rational explanations arrived, including the building of bikes,

that added up and made sense like numbers in chalk.

What was Sethena to make of the large chimney now when she went home?

Already she was using the numbers she'd learned in math, calculating

the cost of two hundred more bricks, more mortar, and more time

that it took for all of them, all of them, to manufacture a Lie.

Stopping Off

You are grabbing grasshoppers
in the car while driving away
with the wildflowers you just
picked from the field
on the right side of 542.

The grasshoppers are jumping out
from daisies and Black-Eyed Susans
and tufts of Goldenrod, all picked
from that field spared by the backhoes
digging a massive hole for the new mall,
where the last of the green clover
closes quietly at night,
a diminishing space where
field mice thrive and multiply
into a world quickly
closing in on itself.

This grabbing of grasshoppers
and driving the car, though,
can't be nearly as dangerous
as making that call

to ensure that you've picked up
the right kind of milk, the right loaf of bread,
or to get home a little late
and to see if you might be able
to make up for lost time
with someone sitting seething
beneath a pretty ceramic vase
etched with faded clovers
and filled with meaningless
plastic flowers.

Poverty, Inc.

A great-great grandmother
in the ghetto
or the rundown suburb
where no one slows to look
or the lonely shack
on the edge of the interstate

has to know

that the falling timber of
rotting walls
and the splinters of
floorboards dropping
into rat-filled basements
goes on forever,

or at least
to the boundary marked
by clean white curbs
beneath glittering buildings
pierced by sunlight,
filled with silk ties,

crystal glasses of brandy
hoisted and clinked, celebrating
the absence
of anything dark, so close
but so a million miles away.

Recycle Day

See the freshly picked pink roses
jutting out of the recycle bin
on top of everything else;
meanwhile the woman on the inside
is weeping still
in early morning.

He can hear her
through the open window
composing broken sobs;
he gathers the handles of the bin,
pushes forward and down,
and drowns out her sobs
with a cascade of their empty bottles:
clinking, crashing, splintering, breaking
into half-collapsed boxes
and the last of the detergent,
all swallowing the pink roses
into the grind.

He would like to believe
the weeping woman on the inside

was like his own ex-wife,
for whom he had bought
freshly picked pink roses
in a final flare of effort
to make the world right again
(he was quickly informed that,
in his choice of final flare,
he had chosen
wrong-colored roses).

Therefore, he was a recycle bin
on recycle day, making noise
beneath her window,
shattered glass,
leaky detergent,
half-collapsed boxes, and
bottles of failed promise,
all capped off with
the wrong-colored roses.

He was dumped, she was dumped,
and he dumps.

The History of Lost Game Shows

He lost on a sports topic
on the final question of *Jeopardy*,
lost by a dollar it turned out.
The answer was *Jim Thorpe*,
on account of his
getting stripped of gold medals
because of money and baseball,
but he had scribbled *golf* instead of a name . . .
and he never golfed again.

She thought the eight-letter word
behind which Vanna was standing
was "e-s-o-t-e-r-i-c"
but there were too many unknown letters
upon which to blindly guess
a word like that, so
she lost in the end
to a man with a blue bow tie—
and she dropped her course work
at the university.

He told Regis he didn't bring his wife
to watch from the audience

"because she is home watching the kids,"
but Regis asked him again
after he passed the first round
why he didn't bring his wife to watch
and in frustration at already having answered,
he yelled at Regis
"because she is home watching the kids . . ."
and then, out of four choices on the next question,
he said J.J. was a sweat hog, then
"down you go" Regis said—
and down went his marriage.

Her sister got her one hundred eighty points
and all he had to do was get twenty points
for twenty thousand dollars
for guessing to Steve what other people might say,
but he answered *acid reflux, bullfrogs, Willy the Pooh, stilts,*
and *lawn mower,*
and the answers made the scoreboard buzz zeroes
and the audience snicker,
except for his sister—
and he stopped attending
the family reunions.

They follow you when you win—
They watch your money as it enters the bank
or while you are driving a fresh black Mercedes
or while you are moving into
the house with the extra rooms.

You appear at restaurants to applause,
you talk about your correct answers,
your timing, your luck, the camera,
forever.

But you are invisible when you lose;
no one pays attention to your answer
of the wrong sport
or because of that wrong answer
you just can't go to the greens now;
or the wrong eight-letter word that
you guessed because
that word was so fascinating to you,
but now you can't study
what only the lonely few know
anymore;
or you couldn't think of Sweathog names
because your wife was angry at you
and stayed home with the kids,
so you stared into a dark audience,
got your sitcoms wrong,
and now she won't be home at all
anymore.

And your sister? She still
harbors hatred for the measly twenty points
you just couldn't get,
twenty points that would at least
have gotten her the shoes and purse

at the top of her list,
on top of her keeping
on top of the rent.
Stupid answers, what were you thinking?
It was so rushed you couldn't think at all and now
you won't fly to your family town
or rent a car or Uber it
to the reunions every summer,
so you won't ever need
to recount memories
of buzzing zeroes
and your lost game.

The Tavern Keeper at the Edge of the World

On the missing tablet
(in the mysterious cave behind the outcropping)
Sidori pours a tall mead for Gilgamesh
to drown the sorrows
of his dead and only friend
but also to have the time
to tell him of her loneliness
on such an empty beach:
it's been so long, so very long
since she's had a patron,
(twenty-two years she counts)
to serve someone like him.

She knows him: through the mead,
lonely Sidori wants to help Gilgamesh forget
the cold and empty mortal world
to which he must return,
forget what he's been told
by his dying and only friend
about the human body
once it's dragged
into the underworld.

It is best to have more mead with me
here at the edge of the known, safe world
and keep me company with the shore,
she tells him as she pours
another and another and another—
until he forgets the beach,
forgets the sea of the dead,
while she finally drinks herself
to forget about the ferryman
waiting on the shore
to take him out
of the hands of mortality
and leave her alone
with the surf once again.

Stay put with me, keep loneliness at bay for me,
she tells him as the waves roll in.
We only have so much time
and so much mead,
so have another with me—
forget your friend, forget
the Great Bull of Heaven
and the coming underworld.
Have another mead with me and
tell me about your fabulous city.

Wanted: One-Inch Baby Jesus

Now that the baby Jesus is missing
it's an existential manger scene where
Mary and Joseph, the three kings,
the lambs, the goats, the cows, and the angels
gather to gawk at a little empty space
in the hay.

It's only a one-inch baby Jesus,
a pewter nugget to match
the other pewter nuggets entering
the ceramic house
with a floor of straw, but it
is impossible to find.

However, a two- inch baby Jesus
found on eBay *could* replace it—
But this would throw the world
of religious proportions out of whack,
predicting a fully- grown Jesus
ten feet tall, wide hands, wide feet,
never accepting nails, never fitting
comfortably on a cross.

And that won't do.

Signal School

I

I pocket-dialed dad yesterday.
He was still in my contacts,
though he died two years ago
almost to the day.
He was there with a lower-case *d*
just before *David* and *Dawn*.

I don't know where dad's device
is stored right now; for sure
the battery must be long- dead.
Perhaps it is buried deep
in one of my sister's drawers
or at the bottom of a basement box
or in a landfill after they threw out
his useless, pointless things.

Wherever it is stored,
I can't help thinking
his phone rang
long past his burial,
cutting off after five rings,

waiting finally for a message
he could never hear, for a message
I could never compose.

II

Drafted into the war,
they sent dad to signal school
where he learned aerial telegraphy
or *wigwag* as he called it when he spoke
at the dinner table— of semaphore,
of forming letters in the air with flags,
and *pretend you are*
ships at sea and you need to know
what's going on because
this is how it would be.

He told us of life aboard a tugboat
in the Pacific. He would stand with his flags
on the slippery deck on a sometimes-violent sea—
but dad is wigwagging now
in front of us on the linoleum,
sweeping hands and imaginary flags
across the table, slowly forming words,
letting all of the ships out there know
what he was given to tell them:
Let us know when you need to be
taken to port, let us know how you need us
to guide you out of the open sea
and into the narrow canals of home.

III

One night after spaghetti dinner
dad went into the junk drawer,
brought out a flashlight
and turned it on.
Pressing the little red button
in the center of the switch,
the light flashed on and off in his hands,
strange pink hands suddenly,
before he turned those bursts of light on us:

this is how you talk in the dark
without speech across open ocean.
Watch the short and long flashes I am sending you
so you can know what I am saying, what
letters of the alphabet I am sending to you,
what words and sentences I am sending to you.
You must wait in the dark open space
and watch for the light of my words
and try to decipher me.

www.ingramcontent.com/pod-product-compliance
Lightning Source LLC
Chambersburg PA
CBHW061504040426
42450CB00008B/1483